Skate Parks

Justin Hocking

The Rosen Publishing Group's
PowerKids Press™
New York

For Matt and Sean

Published in 2006 by The Rosen Publishing Group, Inc.
29 East 21st Street, New York, NY 10010

First Edition

Editors: Melissa Acevedo and Orli Zuravicky
Book Design: Elana Davidian

Photo Credits: Cover, p. 12 (left inset) provided by Team Pain; p. © 4 Getty Images; pp. 4 (inset), 12 Courtesy Wally Hollyday; p. 7 (insets) by Michael James © michaeljamesimage.com; pp. 11, 12 (right inset) www.grindline.com; p. 11 (insets) Photo: Steve R. Gump; p. 15 Alltec Skateparks, Inc./www.alltecskateparks.com; pp. 15, 19 © Site Design Group, Inc./www.sitedesigngroup.com/Site Skateparks, Inc./www.siteskateparks.com; p. 19 (top inset) © Duomo/Corbis; p. 19 (bottom inset) © Royalty-Free/Corbis; p. 20 courtesy of Skatepark of Tampa/www.skateparkoftampa.com.

Library of Congress Cataloging-in-Publication Data

Hocking, Justin.
Skate parks / Justin Hocking.
    p. cm. — (Power skateboarding)
Includes bibliographical references and index.
ISBN 1-4042-3047-5 (library binding)
1. Skateboarding parks—United States—Juvenile literature. I. Title. II. Series.

GV859.8.H625 2006
796.22—dc22
                          2004019746

Manufactured in the United States of America

Contents

Skateboarders used to skate mainly on roads and sidewalks, like the two boys in the above picture from the 1960s. *Inset:* Open from 1978–1981, Cherry Hill Skatepark, in Cherry Hill, New Jersey, was voted the best skate park of the twentieth century.

People first started riding skateboards in the early 1940s. By the mid-1970s, skateboarding had become very popular, and skaters were looking for new challenges. Around this time a man named George Scott came up with the idea of building a park specially **designed** for skateboarding. In 1976, Skateboard City was the first skate park ever built. It was also known as Scatboard City because their logo was the Scat Cat. It was located in Port Orange, Florida. Soon after, Carlsbad Skatepark opened in Carlsbad, California. It was not long before skate parks began appearing all over the country and even in places as far away as Europe and Asia. These early skate parks were made of **concrete**. They usually consisted of different types of **obstacles**. They also featured deep, rounded **pools**.

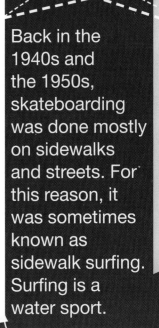

Back in the 1940s and the 1950s, skateboarding was done mostly on sidewalks and streets. For this reason, it was sometimes known as sidewalk surfing. Surfing is a water sport.

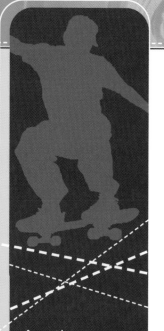

Another famous park, the Pipeline, was located in Uplands, California. Completed in 1977, the Pipeline was known for its very deep pools and large full-pipe.

Though Skateboard City was built first, California's Carlsbad Skatepark became the more famous of the two. Its smooth concrete and many obstacle choices set a standard for later parks. One such park was Cherry Hill Skatepark in New Jersey. It was open from 1978 to 1981 and was one of the largest parks of its time. It was home to a famous giant egg-shaped pool that was said to be one of the best skate pools ever built.

Perhaps the most famous skate park in history was the Del Mar Skate Ranch. It was open from 1978 to 1987 and was located in San Diego, California. It had several pools and **half-pipes**. It was also home to the famous oval Keyhole pool. Many well-known skaters, such as Tony Hawk and Danny Way, grew up riding the Keyhole pool at Del Mar.

Most skate parks have half-pipes, which are ramps shaped like a *U*. The skater above is using a half-pipe ramp to do a trick. *Insets*: A young Tony Hawk rides a half-pipe ramp at the Del Mar Skate Ranch in 1980.

The Louisville Extreme Park, shown above, has 40,000 square feet (3,716 sq m) of concrete skating surface. The park has a full-pipe ramp which is round and shaped like a tube. It also has a wooden vert ramp and a 20,000-square-foot (1,858 sq m) building for indoor skating.

Modern Skate Parks

The early skate parks no longer exist. Places like the Pipeline, Del Mar, and Cherry Hill were privately owned. It became too expensive to keep them open. During the 1990s, there was an increase in the construction of public skate parks all over America. Today hundreds of skate parks exist across the country.

Street skating became popular in the 1990s. Many of today's parks have obstacles one would find on streets, such as **ledges**, curbs, handrails, and staircases. The Newberg Park, in Newberg, Oregon, has 30,000 square feet (2,787 sq m) of pools. It also has snake-runs and other obstacles. The Louisville Extreme Park, in Louisville, Kentucky, is larger than the Newberg Park. Similar to the Pipeline, Louisville Extreme Park includes a 24-foot- (7 m) high **full-pipe** and a **vert ramp**.

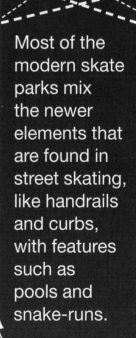

Most of the modern skate parks mix the newer elements that are found in street skating, like handrails and curbs, with features such as pools and snake-runs.

9

Skate Park Designers and Builders

With the increase in the need for public skate parks, several **custom** skate park construction companies have formed. These companies are different from regular construction companies. Their crews are made up of people who have many years of experience riding skateboards and building skate parks. Because they actually skateboard, these highly skilled workers know how to build obstacles that other skaters will enjoy. Specialized skate park builders know that even the tiniest flaw in the park's surface can cause a skater to fall off his or her board. With this in mind, the builders put much care into their wooden and concrete creations. There are more than 20 major custom skate park construction companies right now. These companies include Dreamland Skateparks, Grindline Skateparks, RCMC Custom Cement Skateparks, and Team Pain Skateparks.

Created by Grindline, the Hillyard Skatepark in Spokane, Washington, is 12,000 square feet (1,115 sq m) of smooth concrete. The above picture shows a close-up of the park's ramps and pools. *Insets*: Skaters Sonny Robertson (top) and Tom Miller (bottom) do different tricks on the obstacles in the Newberg Skatepark in Newberg, Oregon.

11

12 The above picture is a design by Wally Hollyday for a Nashville skate park. Hollyday designed and built the Cherry Hill Skatepark in New Jersey. *Left inset:* The construction of a Team Pain ramp. *Right inset:* A skate park is being built.

How Skate Parks Are Built

Before designing a new skate park for a town, most custom skate park builders meet with the town's local skateboarders. This helps give the designers a sense of which obstacles the skate park users would like to skate on the most. After the designers create a plan for what the park will look like, construction of the skate park can begin. The most popular type of skate park is built of concrete. The first step in building a concrete park is digging a large hole in the ground with machines called excavators. Workers then shape wood into the basic form of the park floor and its obstacles. Metal rods called **rebar** are laid out on top of the shaped wood. The rebar will form a metal frame for the park. Workers then pour wet concrete over the rebar and smooth it out using tools. The rebar keeps the concrete together and makes it stronger. After several days the concrete dries and hardens into the shape that the workers created.

Many modern skate parks include a pool in their design. Most of these pools are made of concrete. One of the most famous concrete pools is the very large Combi pool at the Vans Skateboard Park in Orange County, California. "Combi" is short for "combination." Instead of making a simple round pool, the Combi builders combined several round and square pools that are different sizes. Some are deep and some are not. The Combi design allows skaters to do harder tricks than they might do in a regular pool. They can even do tricks from one pool to the other.

The Combi pool's shape has greatly changed skate park pool design. Few pools are as big or as deep as the Combi. However, many public skate parks around the country include pools with a combination-style design. For instance, the pool at the Edora Skatepark in Fort Collins, Colorado, combines an egg-shaped pool with a round pool and a square pool.

This pool from the Encinitas YMCA Skatepark in Encinitas, California, was designed by the Site Design Group. *Inset:* Steve Alba skateboards in a pool in Edora Skatepark in Fort Collins, Colorado. Edora Skatepark was designed by Tim Altic and local skaters.

15

Skateboarders use half-pipe ramps to do tricks. *Top inset:* This wooden half-pipe ramp is located at the Anaheim Pond in Anaheim, California. *Bottom inset:* Lindsi Thompson rides a half-pipe ramp at the 1998 X Games in San Diego, California.

Half-Pipes

Another common skate park feature is the half-pipe. It is a large, U-shaped form created by connecting two ramps with a flat bottom. The Encinitas YMCA Skatepark is home to one of the largest half-pipes in the world. The park is located in Encinitas, California. Made from wood, this half-pipe is a ramp that is 120 feet (37 m) wide and 13 feet (4 m) high, with 2 feet (0.6 m) of pure **vertical** at the top. It also has a 19-foot- (6 m) high roll-in ramp, which lets the skaters enter the half-pipe at a fast speed. The outer surface of the ramp is covered with a strong, weatherproof **material** known as Skatelite.

Many **amateur** skaters also enjoy a smaller form of the half-pipe called the mini ramp. These ramps are usually between 4 feet (1 m) and 6 feet (1.8 m) high. Mini ramps are commonly found at local skate parks.

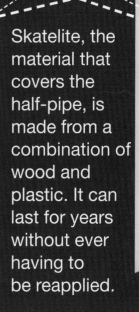

Skatelite, the material that covers the half-pipe, is made from a combination of wood and plastic. It can last for years without ever having to be reapplied.

Most modern skate parks have a street course, which has obstacles like those you might find in the street. Street courses come in all shapes and sizes, with different obstacles such as **pyramids**, ledges, and **flatbars**. The more obstacles a street course has, the more tricks a skater is able to do there. Street courses also need to have a good "flow." This means that the obstacles are laid out in a way that allows the skaters to move easily, or flow, from one to the other.

One of the best street courses is located in the Louisville Extreme Park in Kentucky. It has one of the largest street courses in the country. The street course includes several types of **fun boxes**, flatbars, and rails. It also includes several ledges of different sizes and shapes. These ledges are stacked on top of each other to create an interesting obstacle. It is like one you might find in a public square or other open area in a town or city.

The Site Design Group designed this street course in Kettering, Ohio. The steps and curbs are used as obstacles. *Top inset:* This skater is just coming off of a ramp. *Bottom inset:* The skater shown here uses an obstacle that is commonly found in street courses.

The Skatepark of Tampa in Tampa Bay, Florida, is no ordinary skate park. The park hosts different events and contests throughout the year. All of the above photos were taken at an amateur SPOT contest.

Skate Park Contests

Skaters enter skate park **contests** for fun and prizes. Amateur contests are held at skate parks all over the country. One of the largest and most popular amateur skate contests takes place every January. It is held at the Skatepark of Tampa in Tampa Bay, Florida. The park is called SPOT for short. The SPOT contest started out as a small event, but now more than 200 skaters travel from all over the country to enter.

Most contests run basically the same way. Separate events are held for the street course, half-pipe, and pool. Skaters have two 45-second runs, or chances, for each event. Judges give the skaters scores based on the skaters' riding styles, how hard the skaters' tricks are, and the skaters' ability to stay on their boards. The judges choose the winners based on the best score of their two runs.

First-place winners of the SPOT contest often go on to become professional, or pro, skateboarders. Pro skaters make a living skateboarding.

With so many skilled builders pushing the limits of skate park design, the skate parks of tomorrow will continue to get bigger and better. One trend for new designs is to make skate parks that do not look at all like skate parks. For instance, in Kettering, Ohio, the Site Design Group has created a design for a skate park that will look like a large urban plaza. Things that would be found in an urban plaza will be placed among street-style obstacles. For example, trees and grass will be placed along with ledges and staircases. This type of design appeals to street skaters, who prefer skating in streetlike surroundings. Many new parks will also appeal to skaters who like ramps and **bowls**. The Dreamland Skatepark designers have plans for a skate park called the Monster Park. To get from the Monster Park's top level to the bottom one, skaters will be able to shoot down a twisting ramp. Skateboarders definitely have much to look forward to!

Glossary

amateur (A-muh-tur) Someone who does something as a hobby, for free.

bowls (BOHLZ) Types of pools found at skateparks, usually made of wood.

concrete (KON-kreet) A mix of water, stones, sand, and a special gray powder. Concrete becomes very hard and strong when it dries.

contests (KON-tests) Games or tests.

custom (KUS-tum) To build something the way someone wants it.

designed (dih-ZYND) To have planned the form of something.

flatbars (FLAT-barz) Metal bars used for tricks. Most are about 1 foot (.3 m) high and 8 feet (2.4 m) long.

full-pipe (FUL-pyp) A round tube, usually about 20 feet (6 m) high.

fun boxes (FUN BOKSZ) A box, usually wooden, with surfaces suitable for riding.

half-pipes (HAF-pyps) Two ramps facing each other, with a flat bottom in between them.

ledges (LEJ-iz) Small, square obstacles used for doing tricks.

material (muh-TEER-ee-ul) What something is made of.

obstacles (OB-stih-kulz) Any objects that can be used in a skateboarding trick.

pools (POOLZ) Empty swimming pools used for skateboarding.

pyramids (PEER-uh-midz) Types of obstacles commonly found in skate park street courses. A pyramid is usually a shape with a square base and three triangular sides that meet at the tip, but pyramids in skate parks have flat tops.

rebar (REE-bar) Metal rods that form a frame in the building of skate parks.

street skating (STREET SKAYT-ing) Skating in the streets using obstacles like benches, stairs, handrails, and ledges.

vertical (VER-tih-kul) In an up-and-down direction. Vertical ramps are called vert ramps for short.

vert ramp (VERT RAMP) The largest type of half-pipe, with walls that are completely vertical at the top. Most vert ramps are between 10 feet (3 m) and 13 feet (4 m) high.

Index

Web Sites

Due to the changing nature of Internet links, PowerKids Press has developed an online list of Web sites related to the subject of this book. This site is updated regularly. Please use this link to access the list:
www.powerkidslinks.com/skate/parks/